History

History

Brian Williams

Miles Kelly
PUBLISHING

Author
Brian Williams

Designed, Edited and Project Managed by
Starry Dog Books

Editor
Belinda Gallagher

Assistant Editor
Mark Darling

Artwork Commissioning
Lesley Cartlidge

Indexer
Janet De Saulles

Art Director
Clare Sleven

Editorial Director
Paula Borton

First published in 2001 by
Miles Kelly Publishing Ltd
The Bardfield Centre
Great Bardfield
Essex CM7 4SL

24681097531

Some material in this book can also be found in *The Greatest Book of the Biggest and Best*

Copyright © Miles Kelly Publishing Ltd 2001

1842-360-055-4460

A British Library Cataloguing-in-Publication Data.
A catalogue record for this book is available from the British Library

909

ISBN 1-84236-065-5

Printed in China

www.mileskelly.net
info@mileskelly.net

CONTENTS

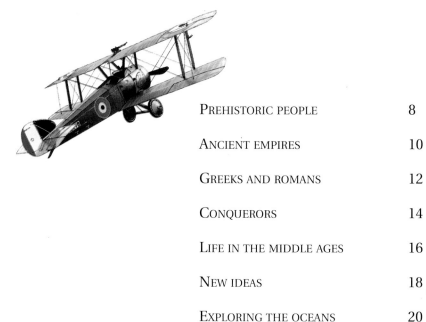

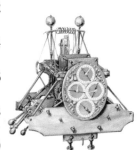

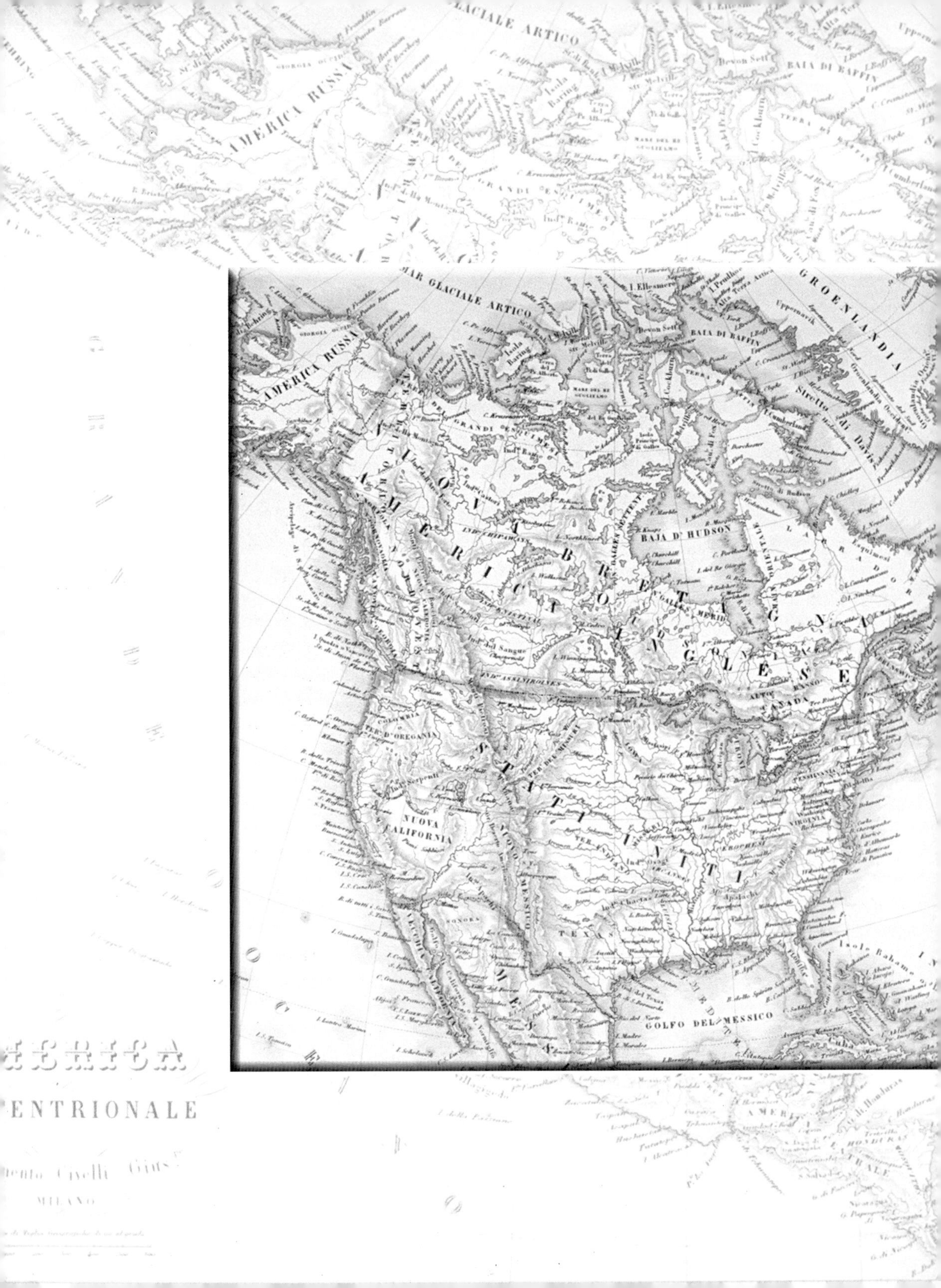

MAR GLACIALE ARTICO
GROENLANDIA
AMERICA RUSSA
BAIA DI BAFFIN
Stretto di Davis
BAJA D' HUDSON
NUOVA CALIFORNIA
TEXAS
GOLFO DEL MESSICO
Isole Bahama
ENTRIONALE
MILANO

HISTORY

History is constantly changing, year by year, month by month, day by day. Since prehistoric times when man first hunted for food, through to the 21st century, age of complex computers, the written word has been one of the most important ways of passing on information.

We know so much about ancient empires, such as the Romans and Greeks, through writings they left behind. Beautiful architecture and monuments reveal how sophisticated these people were, with ideas ahead of their time. Rome had its own form of central heating 2,000 years ago!

Some facts will never change – the discovery of Australia, the first man on the Moon. Others are more mysterious, like the disappearance of the Princes in the Tower, the ghostly face on the Turin shroud. In fact, as you read this introduction, history is being made all around you.

Explore the biggest and best facts of *History* and and you could become a history maker. There are the big, serious facts – for reference – and less serious ones, too, for fun. Packed into these pages are the biggest and best, oddest and strangest, smallest and funniest facts around!

◀ HISTORICAL MAP OF THE UNITED STATES OF AMERICA

PREHISTORIC PEOPLE

Imagine that all the time since the world began (about 4.5 billion years) was just one year. In this imaginary year, there were no people until about 7.40 in the evening on the last day of the year. Human history is a tiny footnote to Earth's history. The first humans hunted animals and gathered wild plants for food. They made stone and bone tools, and later learned to make fire. About 10,000 years ago humans found out how to grow crops. They settled down in villages, which grew into the first cities. Civilization had begun.

▲ *'Otzi the Iceman' died some 5,300 years ago while crossing the mountains between Austria and Italy. His frozen corpse was found in 1991. Although Otzi had been wearing warm winter clothing made from skins, he was unable to survive the cold when he became trapped by heavy snow.*

▼ *This skull belonged to an Australopithecus – someone who lived 3 million years ago and walked upright, like modern humans. In 1974 the almost-complete skeleton of a female Australopithecus, nicknamed Lucy, was found in Ethiopia. She was as tall as a 10-year-old girl, but aged about 40.*

▶ *The first humans used rocks as weapons to kill animals for food. They were slower and weaker than many of the animals they hunted, but using their brains and teamwork they became successful hunters.*

▸ First artists: more than 25,000 years ago   ▸ First farmers: about 10,000 years ago   ▸ First domestic animal: dog

DID YOU KNOW?
The remains of Çatal Hüyük, an 8,000-year-old town, were found in 1958 beneath a grass-covered mound in Turkey. About 5,000 people lived there.

TIMELINE

4 million years ago	*Australopithecus*
2 million years ago	*Homo habilis;* **first stone tools**
1.5 million years ago	*Homo erectus;* **used hand axes and fire**
200,000 years ago	**Neanderthal people; first to bury dead**
100,000 years ago	*Homo sapiens;* **bigger brains than *H. erectus***
40,000 years ago	*Homo sapiens sapiens* **– modern humans**
10,000 years ago	**Farming begins; many stone tools made**
7,000 years ago	**First copper tools**
5,000 years ago	**First bronze tools**
3,500 years ago	**First iron tools**

▲ *People who hunted and gathered food never stayed long in one place. But once humans began to plant crops, they stayed to watch them grow and to harvest them. The first crop that farmers grew was wild wheat, about 10,000 years ago.*

▲ *Fire was the biggest advance made by early prehistoric people. They made fires to keep warm, to give light in the darkness of the night, for cooking meat, and to frighten away wild animals. Stone Age people also made stone tools and used the skins of the animals they hunted to make clothing and tents.*

STEPS TOWARDS CIVILIZATION

	HOMINID (HUMAN) SPECIES	WHEN LIVING
★ 1	*Australopithecus*	4 million years ago
2	*Homo habilis* (handy human)	2 million years ago
3	*Homo erectus* (upright human)	1.5 million years ago
4	*Homo sapiens* (wise human)	100,000 years ago

ANCIENT EMPIRES

Civilization developed close to great rivers, in fertile regions where farmers could plant crops and trade with their neighbours. Villages grew into cities, and people became town-dwellers for the first time. Their leaders became kings, with more power than any leaders before. The strongest kings ruled more than one city, creating the first empires. They led armies into battle, made laws to govern their empires, and were often treated like gods. The first great empire was Egypt, which lasted for almost 3,000 years. But much bigger in area was the Indus Valley civilization. It ended about 1500 BC, either because of floods or invaders.

▲ *The Egyptians built mighty monuments in stone, like these giant figures of King Ramesses II (1289–1224 BC), which guard the temple at Abu Simbel.*

▶ *This clay seal, used to label a merchant's goods, was found in the Indus Valley in present-day Pakistan, where a rich civilization flourished some 4,500 years ago.*

» GREAT EMPIRES AND RULERS
Egypt
Sumer, Mesopotamia
Indus Valley civilization, Indian sub-continent
Babylonia
Ur, Mesopotamia
Minoan civilization, Crete
China (beginning of Shang power)
Mycenean civilization, Greece and Turkey
Assyria

◀ *Ancient empires, such as those of Egypt and Assyria, grew larger and more powerful by conquering neighbouring empires. New weapons, such as the fast, horse-drawn chariot, gave their armies an advantage over the enemy. One man steered the vehicle, while an archer shot at the enemy, who were on foot.*

First writing: cuneiform » Best at maths: Babylonians » First iron users: Hittites » First laws: Hammurabi of Babylon's

▲ Carved stone heads higher than a person stand as monuments to the Olmecs, a people who lived in Mexico about 2,500 years ago. Their civilization may have been the first great civilization in North America.

TIMELINE	
8000 BC	Farming begins in the Near East;
	Jericho is built – one of the first cities
6500 BC	Oldest-known woven textiles, from Turkey
5000 BC	Farming in Egypt and China
3500 BC	Sumerians invent writing and the wheel
2000 BC	Start of the Assyrian Empire
1766 BC	Beginning of Shang power in China
1450 BC	Volcano wrecks Minoan palaces on Crete
1250 BC	Greeks capture Troy, according to legend
1200 BC	Rise of Olmec power in Mexico
221 BC	Shih Huangdi is first emperor of all China

3100 to 30 BC	United under King Menes
4000 to 2000 BC	Greatest ruler, Sargon of Akkad
2500 to 1500 BC	No rulers known
1800 to 500 BC	Great kings Hammurabi and Nebuchadnezzar II
2100 BC (strongest)	Under King Ur-Nammu
2000–1100 BC	Named after legendary King Minos
1766 BC	Empire united by Shih Huangdi in 221 BC
1600–1100 BC	Greatest ruler, Agamemnon
800 BC (at its peak)	Last great king, Assurbanipal

► The Sumerians invented writing about 5,500 years ago. Called cuneiform, meaning 'wedge-shaped', it was made by pressing wedge-shaped 'pens' onto soft clay.

► Babylon in Mesopotamia (modern Iraq) was the capital of the Babylonian Empire. In 605 BC King Nebuchadnezzar II enlarged the city and built a magnificent new entrance, called the Ishtar Gate, in the city's northern wall. The blue-tiled gate stood 15 m tall. Babylonia conquered Assyria in 612 BC, but in 539 BC Babylon fell to Cyrus the Great of Persia.

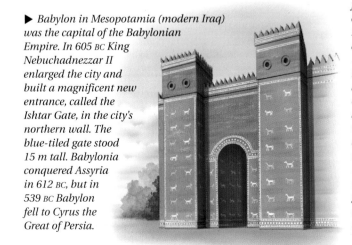

► These life-sized clay soldiers, buried in the tomb of the first Chinese emperor, Shih Huangdi, and discovered in 1974, gave historians an accurate picture of the clothes and weapons of the time. The emperor went to the grave with 10,000 model warriors to guard him in the next world.

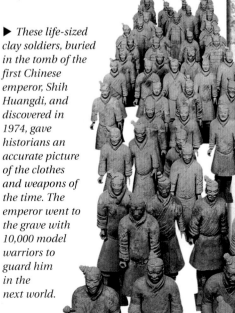

GREEKS AND ROMANS

Greece and Rome shaped the Western world, through language, art and political ideas. Ancient Greece was not one country, but many quarrelsome city-states. It produced many famous writers, thinkers and scientists. Greek civilization reached its height in the 400s BC. In 146 BC Greece was conquered by the Roman Empire. The Romans, originally farmers from central Italy, adopted many Greek customs and gods. They conquered most of Europe and North Africa, and by AD 100 Rome ruled the biggest empire in the Western world.

▲ *Greek foot-soldiers won many battles by advancing in a formation called a* phalanx. *Each man had a round shield and a long spear, and as the* phalanx *charged, it presented a bristling array of spearpoints.*

▼ *The Greeks were great seafarers. Traders explored the islands and bays of the Mediterranean Sea in cargo boats like this one, founding colonies along the way. The explorer Pytheas even sailed as far north as Britain.*

◀ *One of the most famous Greek scientists was Archimedes (287–212 BC). His 'bathwater-test' proved a king's crown was not pure gold. The crown displaced more water than a piece of pure gold that weighed the same as the crown.*

MOST FAMOUS ANCIENT GREEKS	
Pericles	The wisest ruler of Athens
Alexander the Great	The greatest soldier to come out of Greece
Homer	The most famous poet
Socrates	A philosopher, forced to kill himself
Aristotle	A great scientist and thinker

▶ *The legendary war between Greece and Troy, a city in Turkey, lasted for 10 years. The Greeks finally tricked their way into Troy by hiding soldiers inside a wooden horse, which the Trojans dragged into their city.*

◀ *The Roman Empire at its peak, about AD 100, ruled Britain to the north of Rome, Spain to the west, Palestine to the east and North Africa to the south.*

▶ *A Roman legionary soldier was a well-disciplined, full-time professional. On the march he wore armour and carried a shield, javelin and sword, tools for making camp, and his kit slung from a pole.*

▼ *The centre of government of the Roman Empire was the Forum in Rome, which was originally a market place. It had imposing temples and public buildings, including the Senate, of which only ruins remain.*

▼ *In 218 BC Hannibal, the Carthaginian general, led an army against Rome. He took his troops, with their war elephants, across the Alps in a daring attack, but in the end he, and Carthage, were defeated.*

▶▶ MOST FAMOUS ROMANS

Julius Caesar	General, almost became king but was murdered
Augustus	First emperor and winner of civil wars
Mark Antony	Soldier, fell in love with Cleopatra, queen of Egypt
Hadrian	Emperor, famous for his wall in northern Britain
Constantine	First Christian emperor, AD 324–337

TIMELINE

753 BC	Traditional date for founding of Rome
700 BC	Greek poet Homer composes the *Iliad* and *Odyssey*
509 BC	Rome becomes a republic, its last king overthrown
500s BC	Greeks invent democracy
490–431 BC	Greeks defeat Persians; golden age of Athens
438 BC	Parthenon temple in Athens completed
336 BC	Alexander the Great becomes ruler of Macedon
200s BC	Romans defeat Carthage (a rival state in North Africa)
146 BC	Greece comes under Roman control
49 BC	Julius Caesar rules as dictator in Rome
27 BC	End of Roman Republic and start of Roman Empire
AD 98–117	Roman Empire at its greatest, under Emperor Trajan
AD 286	Empire divided into Eastern and Western parts
AD 476	End of Western Empire; Eastern continues as Byzantium

CONQUERORS

History's great conquerors were men of great ambition and determination. They had the support of well-trained soldiers to back them up – soldiers like the Roman legionary, the Norman knight in chain mail armour, the fast-riding Mongol archer and Napoleon's Imperial Guard, marching in ranks with muskets at the ready. Of all the great conquerors in history, none was more feared than the 12th-century Mongol leader Genghis Khan. His horsemen conquered a vast empire extending across Asia from China as far west as the Danube River in Europe.

▶ *Babur (1483–1530) was the great Muslim leader who conquered India in 1526 by defeating Ibrahim, the Sultan of Delhi, at Panipat. Babur made himself emperor of India.*

▼ *Cyrus the Great was the 6th-century ruler of Persia. He founded an empire extending from the Mediterranean to India, uniting peoples in the region by conquest. Cyrus died in 529 BC and was buried in this huge tomb.*

▲ *One thousand Spanish troops, led by Hernando Cortés, conquered the Aztec Empire in Mexico in the three years from 1519 to 1521. Spanish guns, armour and horses, together with Indian allies, proved too strong for the Aztec armies.*

▼ *Napoleon was France's most ambitious general. He dreamt of building an empire bigger than Rome's. In 1812 he reached Moscow, but finding the city on fire he ordered his Grand Army to retreat. The freezing winter came early and devastated his troops. Defeat in Russia marked the beginning of his fall.*

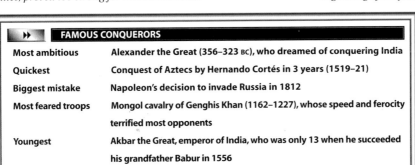

▶▶ FAMOUS CONQUERORS	
Most ambitious	Alexander the Great (356–323 BC), who dreamed of conquering India
Quickest	Conquest of Aztecs by Hernando Cortés in 3 years (1519–21)
Biggest mistake	Napoleon's decision to invade Russia in 1812
Most feared troops	Mongol cavalry of Genghis Khan (1162–1227), whose speed and ferocity terrified most opponents
Youngest	Akbar the Great, emperor of India, who was only 13 when he succeeded his grandfather Babur in 1556

➤ Most ruthless: Spanish conquistadors ➤ Shortest: Napoleon ➤ Most feared: Genghis Khan ➤ Youngest: Akbar, 13

◀ *Genghis Khan conquered the biggest land empire in history. A tribal ruler at the age of 13, he led his armies to defeat China by 1212. After this his generals extended his rule as far west as the Middle East and Russia.*

TIMELINE	
330 BC	Alexander conquers the Persian Empire
44 BC	The Romans invade Britain
AD 715	Muslims from North Africa conquer Spain
800	Charlemagne controls western Europe
1066	The Normans conquer England
1100s	The Khmers conquer Southeast Asia
1200s	Genghis Khan conquers much of Asia
1279	Kublai Khan (grandson of Genghis) conquers China
1397	Tamerlane (Mongol) invades India
1521	Cortés of Spain conquers the Aztecs of Mexico
1526	Babur founds the Mogul Empire in India
1536	Pizarro of Spain conquers the Incas of Peru
1804	Napoleon controls most of Europe

▶ *The best-known conqueror is probably Alexander the Great. In a short but astonishing life, he conquered Persia, Babylon and Egypt, and invaded India. Ferocious energy drove him on, but in India his exhausted troops begged him to return home.*

▶ *Charlemagne, king of the Franks in Gaul (modern France), was crowned western Europe's new Roman emperor in AD 800. His empire covered France, Germany and Italy as far south as Rome. Often called the perfect ruler, his main aim was to spread Christianity.*

LIFE IN THE MIDDLE AGES

The Middle Ages were dangerous, but creative times. Some of Europe's most magnificent cathedrals were built in praise of God, and beautiful hand-painted or 'illuminated' Bibles were made by the monks in Europe's many monasteries. Dangers included disease such as the Black Death, which killed about one quarter of Europe's population. Wars were also frequent, as powerful rulers attempted to extend their territories or assert control. The Crusades, for example, lasted on and off for hundreds of years. Punishments for disobeying the Church were severe, and included being burned at the stake.

▲ Medieval towns were over-crowded, and drains ran along the narrow, dirty streets. Cooking fires often set light to the wooden houses, and whole towns – such as Rouen in France – sometimes burned down.

◀ Most people in medieval times were peasants, who farmed the land for the lord of a manor. They also grew food for themselves. The poorest peasants were not free, but had to obey the lord.

» PAINFUL PUNISHMENTS FOR LAWBREAKERS
Being burned alive, the usual punishment for witchcraft
Having your ears or hands cut off and your nose slit
Being dragged around town with rotting fish hung round your neck
Sitting in the stocks (a wooden trap) and being pelted with rubbish
Whipping, hanging, beheading – nobles could choose beheading

◀ Rats were a great menace. They not only ate food stores, but also carried the Black Death, or plague.

◀ A tournament was the biggest sporting event in the medieval calendar. Knights, the most important medieval soldiers, charged at one another with lances, testing their skill at knocking their opponent to the ground. From about 1400, the knights wore suits of plate armour.

Lowliest workers: peasants »» Biggest residences: castles »» Greatest engineering feats: cathedrals

▲ *The biggest building projects of the Middle Ages were castles and cathedrals. Some cathedrals took hundreds of years to complete. The craftsmen shown here are making a round cathedral window.*

TIMELINE	
529	**First abbey in Europe, at Monte Cassino, Italy**
700s	**Start of feudal system in western Europe**
1066	**Normans conquer England**
1096	**First Crusade or holy war for control of the Holy Land**
1249	**Britain's first university, Oxford University**
1260	**Hanseatic League of trading cities founded**
1265	**First real parliament in England**
1270	**Last Crusade**
1300s	**First use of gunpowder and cannon in war**
1337–1453	**Hundred Years' War between England and France**
1348	**Black Death reaches England; all Europe is affected**

▼ *Some of the biggest medieval abbeys were in France. Cluny Abbey was founded in 910. Its church or basilica, shown here, was the largest in the world until the completion of St Peter's in Rome.*

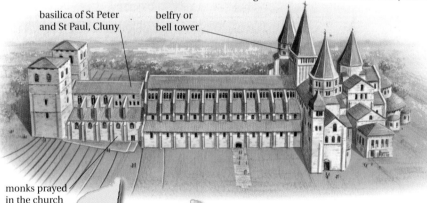

basilica of St Peter and St Paul, Cluny

belfry or bell tower

monks prayed in the church at set hours of the day and night

▼ *Medieval battles were often confused and bloody affairs, fought with bows, swords, spears and spiked clubs. At Bannockburn in 1314, the Scots under Robert Bruce beat Edward II's much larger English army with its formidable knights in armour on their great warhorses.*

PIGS AT LARGE!

● Pigs were a nuisance in medieval towns. Many people kept pigs in their backyards or in alleyways. A law was passed so that any pig found wandering could be 'arrested'. The pig's owner had to pay four pennies to get it back.

NEW IDEAS

The greatest explosion of new ideas in Europe came in the 1400s, a period called the Renaissance, or 'rebirth'. It was a period during which ancient knowledge was rediscovered, and new ideas in art and science were spread by the new invention of printing. By the 1700s this 'age of Enlightenment' had sparked off a revolution in science and technology – the Industrial Revolution – which changed the way people lived and worked. Ideas about politics also changed, bringing new ways of government.

▶ *Michael Faraday (1791–1867) had little schooling, but a brilliant mind. He rose to become a professor of chemistry, and his new ideas led to the invention of the electric motor and electrical generator.*

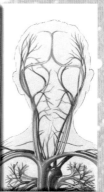

◀ *Andreas Vesalius (1514–64), a Flemish (Belgian) scientist, wrote the first book on anatomy to show detailed drawings of the inside of the human body. He also dissected corpses as a way of teaching medical students – a startling idea in the 1500s.*

◀ *Leonardo da Vinci (1452–1519) was a genius far ahead of his time. He drew plans for amazing new machines, such as aircraft similar to this first helicopter, as well as armoured cars and submarines.*

▼ *New ideas about machines and making goods in factories brought about the Industrial Revolution of the 1700s and 1800s. With the changes in living and working conditions came new ideas about public health and education.*

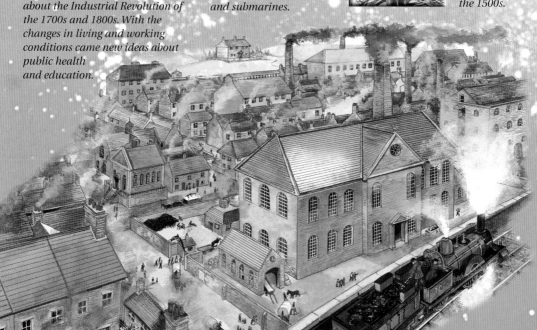

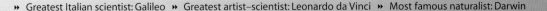

▲ *Florence Nightingale, known as the 'lady with the lamp', upset the British army during the Crimean War (1854–56) by voicing new ideas about the way wounded soldiers should be cared for, and demanding changes in nursing practice.*

▼ *One of the biggest new ideas of the 19th century was Charles Darwin's theory of evolution, published in 1859 in his book* Origin of Species. *After visiting the remote Galapagos Islands, Darwin realized that the animals there had 'evolved' over a long period as they competed for food, and that only the fittest survived.*

TIMELINE	
1265	Roger Bacon at work on an encyclopedia of knowledge
c.1266	Giotto born – great Renaissance artist of 'lifelike' pictures
1452	Leonardo da Vinci, artist and inventor, is born in Italy
1513	Macchiavelli writes *The Prince*, about the ideal ruler
1543	Copernicus's new idea – that Earth moves around the Sun
1550	Gutenberg invents printing with movable type
1609	Galileo studies the Moon through his telescope
1642	Pascal invents an adding machine
1667	Newton publishes his laws of gravity and motion
1701	Tull invents the first seed drill to help farmers
1709	Darby discovers how to produce iron cheaply
1782	Watt makes the first efficient steam engine

THE GALAPAGOS ISLANDS

▲ *Some ideas are hard to accept, others to understand. Copernicus's idea that Earth moves around the Sun was rejected by the Christian Church in the 15th century. Astronomers today are trying to work out just how old and big the Universe is – a concept most of us will never really grasp!*

››	PEOPLE WHOSE IDEAS CHANGED THE WAY WE SEE THE WORLD	
Copernicus	1473–1543	Polish astronomer who upset ancient ideas of how the Universe works
John Locke	1632–1704	English philosopher who declared that all men were free and equal
Sir Isaac Newton	1642–1727	English scientist whose ideas about light, motion and gravity revolutionized science
François Voltaire	1694–1778	French writer who criticised the Church and government
Antoine Lavoisier	1743–94	French scientist and founder of modern chemistry
Charles Darwin	1809–82	English naturalist whose ideas about the evolution of life shocked many people

EXPLORING THE OCEANS

The Egyptians led the way in sea voyaging, followed by the Phoenicians, who sailed out of the Mediterranean and into the Atlantic, navigating by the stars. The Chinese sailed large fleets west across the Indian Ocean to Africa, but they never rounded its tip. Meanwhile the Portuguese worked their way down the west coast of Africa and eventually sailed eastwards all the way to India. For early ocean explorers, calm seas were one of the greatest dangers. With no wind, their ships went nowhere and precious supplies ran out.

◀ *In 1735 John Harrison invented the chronometer, a sea clock that helped sailors navigate safely. Without knowing the time, a sailor could not work out how far a ship had sailed.*

▶ *Viking longships were seaworthy enough to cross oceans. They sailed from Scandinavia to Iceland, then crossed the Atlantic to Greenland. From there an expedition, led by a Viking named Leif Ericsson, sailed farther west to North America, landing in AD 1000.*

▶▶ GREATEST SEA EXPLORERS	
Cook	Sailed farther than anyone had before him
Magellan	Lesser men would have turned back
Dias	Voyage into the unknown lasted over 14 months
Columbus	Made four Atlantic voyages; never gave up
Tasman	Survived fierce storms in the Southern Ocean

▶ *In 1492 Christopher Columbus sailed from Spain to the Bahamas. By sailing west across the Atlantic Ocean, he had expected to land on the coast of Asia. Instead, he rediscovered North America.*

◀ *During the 1400s the Chinese, led by an admiral named Cheng Ho, sent large fleets of ocean-going junks across the Indian Ocean to trade with Arabia and East Africa. Had they rounded the tip of Africa, they might have met the Portuguese sailing down the west coast in their quest for a route to India.*

» Most stubborn: Columbus » Unluckiest: Magellan » Biggest health risk: scurvy » Most useful navigation aid: compass

TIMELINE

3000 BC	Egyptians explore Mediterranean Sea
400s BC	Hanno of Carthage sails along west coast of Africa
1405–33	Cheng Ho of China sails as far west as the Persian Gulf
1487–88	Bartolomeu Dias of Portugal sails to southern tip of Africa
1492	Christopher Columbus sails from Spain to the Caribbean
1497	Vasco da Gama of Portugal sails around Africa to India
1497	John Cabot sails from England to North America
1499	Amerigo Vespucci sails to America (named after him)
1519–22	Sebastian del Cano sails around the world
1534	Jacques Cartier discovers the St Lawrence River, Canada
1640s	Abel Tasman of Holland sails to Tasmania
1768	James Cook sets out on the first of three Pacific voyages

▶ *Ferdinand Magellan led the first voyage around the world (1519–22). Magellan was killed in the Philippines, but one of his ships completed the return journey back to Spain.*

▼ *Thousands of years before sailors from the West discovered sea routes around the world, the Polynesians had crossed the Pacific Ocean and found numerous small islands. Ancient stories suggest they sailed in large, twin-hulled canoes.*

▲ *One of the greatest sea explorers ever was Captain James Cook. He made three long voyages of scientific discovery in the 1700s. On a visit to Australia, his crew reported seeing creatures they described as 'jumping dogs' – they were kangaroos!*

KEY TO MAP ROUTES

━━━ 1492 Christopher Columbus sails from Spain to the Bahamas

▦▦▦ 1497–98 Vasco da Gama sails from Portugal to India

━━━ 1519–22 Magellan's round-the-world voyage, completed by del Cano

▪▪▪▪ 1768–71 James Cook explores the Pacific and lands in Australia

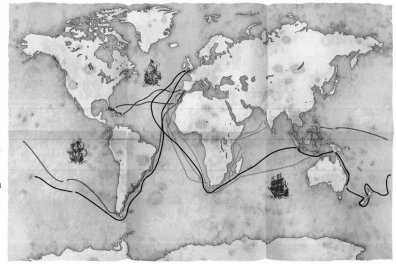

→ Biggest win for archers: Agincourt, 1415 → Biggest American victory over British: Yorktown, 1781

BLOODY BATTLES

In ancient times, armies were small and most battles were settled in an hour or two. Roman soldiers were so well trained that they lost very few battles in more than 500 years. The biggest change in war came in the 1300s, with the first use of cannon and gunpowder. In 1453 the Turks used a monster cannon to fire seven shots a day against the walls of Constantinople. Sixty oxen were needed to drag it! By the 1800s muskets, rifles and machine guns made battles much more destructive. Rapid-firing guns mowed down even the bravest soldiers. The longest war in history was the Hundred Years' War (which actually lasted for 115 years) between Britain and France.

▲ *British infantry under Wellington fired musket volleys at Napoleon's French army during the Battle of Waterloo in 1815. The British and their Prussian allies won.*

▶ *Britain's most famous naval hero is Admiral Horatio Nelson. Despite losing an eye and an arm in earlier battles, he led his fleet to victory against the French and Spanish at Trafalgar in 1805.*

◀ *The best weapon of the Middle Ages was the longbow, used by English and Welsh archers. It was quicker to shoot than the crossbow, and could put an arrow through a wooden shield. Archers helped England win the Battle of Agincourt (1415) against the French.*

▲ *In 1588 the Spanish Armada, a fleet of 130 ships, sailed north to invade England. But not even this mighty fleet could survive cannons, fireships and savage storms – many galleons sank.*

▶▶ GREAT COMMANDERS	
Alexander	Never lost a battle, even against much bigger armies than his own
Napoleon	Expert at using artillery and choosing the right moment to attack
Wellington	Good at choosing when and where to fight, and win
Lee	Led outnumbered Confederate (Southern) armies against Union (Northern) armies in the American Civil War

◀ *Ulysses S Grant (1822–85) was a Union general in the American Civil War, masterminding the defeat of the Confederacy (Southern states). He later became US President (1869–77).*

▲ *Knights seldom charged into battle – they were too heavy – but they usually had a crushing impact on lines of foot-soldiers. At Agincourt, however, in 1415, the French knights were crowded together on boggy ground, which made them easy targets for the English archers.*

TIMELINE		
480 BC	Salamis	Greeks defeat Persians in naval battle
431 BC	Gaugamela	Alexander defeats the Persians
AD 732	Tours	Franks defeat Muslim Saracens
1066	Hastings	Normans beat the English
1346	Crécy	English victorious over the French
1415	Agincourt	English defeat the French
1588	Armada	Spanish invasion fleet destroyed by English
1709	Poltava	Russians beat Swedes
1757	Plassey	British seize control of India
1759	Quebec	British win Canada from the French
1781	Yorktown	Americans beat the British
1805	Trafalgar	British fleet defeats French and Spanish
1815	Waterloo	British and Allies defeat the French
1863	Gettysburg	Union army beats Confederates in American Civil War
1870	Sedan	Germans defeat the French

▲ *Battles of the American Civil War (1861–65) were fought mainly with cannon and rifles. About 620,000 soldiers were killed during the war – half fell in battles, the rest died from disease.*

WORLD AT WAR

World War I (1914–18) was the first truly mechanized war, yet there was very little movement. Pinned down by gunfire, armies became bogged down in defensive trenches, and thousands of soldiers died trying to cross a few metres of muddy ground. World War II (1939–45) was a much bigger war. Few regions of the globe escaped the fighting between the Allies and the German–Japanese Axis forces, and many cities were devastated by bombs.

▲ Hundreds of Allied soldiers, including these US troops, stormed the beaches of German-occupied France from landing craft during the D-Day invasion of 1944. The invasion began the liberation of France.

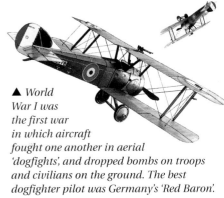

▲ World War I was the first war in which aircraft fought one another in aerial 'dogfights', and dropped bombs on troops and civilians on the ground. The best dogfighter pilot was Germany's 'Red Baron'.

▲ During World War I, German and Allied forces gained ground through trench warfare. In just one battle, the Somme, more than 1 million soldiers were killed going 'over the top' of the trenches into enemy fire.

▶ The Vietnam War (1957–75) was the most controversial of modern wars. America used helicopter 'gunships' to back up their ground troops, but despite their superior firepower they failed to win a final victory.

▶▶	KEY BATTLES OF WORLD WAR II			
Battle of Britain	1940	England	Britain's RAF defeats German air force
Coral Sea	1942	Pacific	US aircraft carriers defeat Japanese fleet
Alamein	1942	North Africa	Allies beat Germans and Italians
Stalingrad	1942–43	Russia	Germans fail to capture Russian city
Normandy	1944	France	Allies invade across English Channel

▲ The mightiest naval warships of the modern era are the US navy's giant nuclear-powered aircraft carriers. During World War II, aircraft carriers with jets became the most effective naval ships.

▼ Tanks such as this one first crawled into battle in 1916, during World War I. The most useless tank was the German 'Mighty Mouse' of 1944, which weighed 190 tonnes. It was very slow and cracked roads as it lumbered along.

TIMELINE

1914	World War I begins – Germany invades France
1916	Battle of the Somme in France; first use of tanks
1916	Naval Battle of Jutland between British and German fleets
1917	USA enters World War I
1918	Germany is defeated; World War I ends
1930	Rise of Nazis in Germany under Adolf Hitler
1937	Japan invades China
1939	World War II begins – Germany invades Poland
1940	France falls to Germany; Battle of Britain
1941	Japanese attack Pearl Harbor; USA joins the Allies
1942	Germans defeated at El Alamein; Japan captures Singapore
1943	Germans defeated at Battle of Stalingrad
1944	First German V-2 rockets; D-Day invasion of France by Allies
1945	Germany surrenders; USA drops two atomic bombs on Japan; Japan surrenders

steel armour protected the tank crew from gunfire

BOMBS

● During World War II, new weapons were invented such as flying bombs and V-2 rockets.

● The war ended when the USA dropped two atomic bombs on Hiroshima and Nagasaki in Japan in 1945.

caterpillar tracks enabled tanks to climb over trench walls and crawl through thick mud

PIONEERS AND TRAILBLAZERS

Pioneers were explorers who set out to cross previously unexplored land, sea or air. They led the way, blazing a trail – or marking the way – for others to follow. Sometimes pioneers were in a race with others to reach the goal first. When Captain Scott reached the South Pole in 1912, for example, he found Amundsen's Norwegian flag already there. The modern age of exploration began about 1800. Since then, for the first time people have crossed the United States, explored Africa, climbed the Himalayas, flown across the oceans, and travelled into space. The whole world is now mapped from space, and there are few places where people have not been.

▲ *Explorer David Livingstone (1813–73) was the first European to see Victoria Falls in central Africa. He later disappeared, but was found in 1871 by Henry Morton Stanley (shown here) in Uganda.*

◀ *America's Amelia Earhart was the most famous pioneer aviator, or flier, of the 1930s. She flew the Atlantic solo in 1932, but disappeared in 1937 while crossing the Pacific on a round-the-world flight.*

▸▸ AMERICAN TRAILBLAZERS	
Daniel Boone	1769
Meriwether Lewis, William Clark	1804–06
Jedediah Smith	1820s
Jim Bridger	1820s
Kit Carson, Charles Frémont	1840s

tobacco

sweet potatoes

sugar cane

pineapple

gold

▲ *The biggest wagon trains rolled west across America from the 1840s. A group of a thousand settlers set out for Oregon in 1843, crossing difficult terrain and Native-American territories. Thousands more pioneers headed for California after gold was found there in 1848.*

◀ *Pioneers in America often hoped to 'get rich quick' by finding gold. Others settled for selling new products, such as tobacco, or became 'planters', growing pineapples, sugar cane or other crops.*

▼ *In 1911–12 two teams of explorers braved icy Antarctica. The team led by Roald Amundsen of Norway (bottom) reached the South Pole first. Robert F Scott's British five-man party (below) arrived a month later, but died from exhaustion while returning.*

LUCKY 13

● Intrepid astronauts had the biggest space escape in April 1970, after the US *Apollo 13* craft was damaged by an explosion on its way to the Moon. Squashed into the tiny Moon lander, with most systems shut down to save power, the astronauts flew round the Moon and back to Earth, and a safe splashdown.

TIMELINE

1271	Marco Polo sets out for China, returning to Venice in 1295
1500s	Spanish gold-seekers explore Central America
1620	*Mayflower* pilgrims land in America
1788	First British settlers land in Australia
1804–06	Lewis and Clark map the American West; new settlers come
1854–56	Livingstone crosses Africa and sees the Victoria Falls
1860	Burke and Wills cross Australia from south to north
1903	First flight in an aeroplane, by the Wrights
1911	Amundsen reaches the South Pole
1953	Hillary and Tenzing climb Everest
1957–58	First overland crossing of Antarctica
1960	Bathyscaphe *Trieste* dives to bottom of the Pacific Ocean
1961	Gagarin circles Earth in a spacecraft
1969	Armstrong and Aldrin are the first people on the Moon

▶ *In 1271 Marco Polo, aged 17, left Venice in Italy with his father and uncle to journey to China, following the ancient Silk Road. It took them three years to reach China. Marco Polo worked for Kublai Khan for 18 years before finally returning to Venice, after 24 years away.*

HEROES AND VILLAINS

National heroes are often fighters – people who saved their country from powerful enemies. William Tell gained heroic status in Switzerland for fighting the Austrians, as did Joan of Arc in France for defeating the English. Another kind of hero is someone who risks their own life to save others. Sometimes the distinction between a hero and a villain is blurred. Ned Kelly, for example, was Australia's most notorious outlaw, but he became a folk hero, like the legendary Robin Hood.

▲ *Lenin (left) became leader of Russia's new Communist government in 1917, after the Revolution. When he died in 1924, he was regarded in Russia as a hero. His successor, Josef Stalin (right), ruled until 1953 as a ruthless dictator, sending millions of people to jail, exile or death.*

▲ *Mohandas K Gandhi (1869–1948), known as the Mahatma ('Great Soul'), led India's struggle for independence from British rule. He always urged non-violence, even when being attacked.*

▼ *One of Scotland's national heroes is William Wallace, the 'Braveheart' of legend. He led his men in battles against the English army of King Edward I, but was eventually captured and put to death in 1305.*

▲ *George Washington (1732–99) is a national hero in America for his generalship in the Revolutionary War, and his wisdom as first president of the United States.*

▲ *Argentina's Che Guevara was a Communist who helped Fidel Castro's revolution in Cuba (1959). He tried to start revolutions in Africa and South America. Killed in Bolivia in 1967, he was 'immortalized' on posters.*

»	NATIONAL HEROES
Joan of Arc	France
George Washington	United States
Simon Bolivar	Bolivia
Giuseppe Garibaldi	Italy
Nelson Mandela	South Africa
Martin Luther King	United States
Mahatma Gandhi	India
Horatio Nelson	Britain
William Tell	Switzerland
William Wallace	Scotland

▲ *American gang-boss Al Capone (1898–1947), one of the worst criminals of the 20th century, controlled a violent crime empire from 1925 to 1931. He was 'Public Enemy No.1', accused of at least 300 murders, but never convicted. Capone was finally jailed for eight years, for not paying his taxes.*

◄ *The 'mad monk' Grigori Rasputin (1871–1916) gained a strange power over Russia's last emperor, Tsar Nicholas II, and Empress Alexandra, who thought him a holy man. But Rasputin led a corrupt life, meddled in politics, and was murdered by Russian noblemen.*

► *Adolf Hitler (1889–1945) was the worst villain of the 20th century. He ruled Germany from 1933 as leader of the Nazi Party, and planned to take over most of Europe. His schemes led to World War II and the Holocaust – the deaths of over 6 million Jews and other people in concentration camps. Facing defeat, Hitler killed himself in 1945.*

▲ *An English hero, possibly based on fact, is the outlaw archer Robin Hood of old English stories. With a band of outlaws from Sherwood Forest (including Friar Tuck and Little John, shown here) he helped the poor against King John and his tax collectors.*

REFORMERS AND REVOLUTIONARIES

Throughout history, people have fought to change bad laws or to help the weak, sick or underprivileged. Great religious reformers included Martin Luther, a German monk who helped start the Reformation or Protestant movement in the 1500s. In the 1700s and 1800s there were many social reformers who sought to modernize nursing, bring an end to child-labour and make prisons more humane. Some reformers tried to change the structure of society, such as Karl Marx, whose writings inspired the Communist revolutions in Russia, China and Cuba in the 20th century.

▲ This painting shows American colonial leaders signing the Declaration of Independence on July 4, 1776. The historic document states that all men are created equal. It created a new nation, the United States of America.

▶ Fidel Castro, a Cuban lawyer, led a Communist uprising that overthrew the government of Cuba in 1959. Castro turned the island of Cuba into a Communist state, and for the rest of the 20th century he defied all America's attempts to unseat him from power. Castro remained an old-style Communist, surviving even the collapse of communism in Russia, which had backed him for years.

▲ From the 1800s, more and more women demanded the same rights as men. In Britain the 'suffragettes' were led by Emmeline Pankhurst (1858–1928) and her daughters. Women chained themselves to railings as part of their campaign for the vote ('suffrage').

▶▶ FIGHTERS FOR THEIR FAITH

Saint Boniface	about 675–754	English missionary to Germany, killed by pagans
Saint Francis of Assisi	1182–1226	Gave up worldly comforts to preach in poverty
Dietrich Bonhoeffer	1906–45	German churchman who opposed the Nazis and was executed
Martin Luther King Jr	1929–68	American Civil Rights leader who was murdered
Janani Luwum	1922–77	Ugandan churchman, killed for opposing the tyrant Idi Amin
Oscar Romero	1917–80	Archbishop of El Salvador, killed for speaking against the government

19TH-CENTURY REFORMERS

- Johann Pestalozzi and Thomas Barnardo cared for orphaned and homeless children.
- John Howard and Elizabeth Fry improved conditions in prisons.
- Henri Dunant founded the Red Cross in 1864.
- Elizabeth Garret Anderson was Britain's first woman doctor in 1875.
- Harriet Tubman and Booker T Washington fought for black Civil Rights.

▲ *Harriet Tubman (1820–1913), a slave in the American South, guided many black slaves to freedom in the North, and later started schools for black people.*

▼ *The Russian Revolution of 1917 grew out of protests by the Russian people against poverty and backwardness, a weak tsar (emperor) and defeats in World War I. The government collapsed, troops and workers took to the streets, and a Communist group called the Bolsheviks, led by Lenin, seized power. The Communist 'Soviet Union' lasted until 1991.*

▲ *Karl Marx (1818–83) was a German thinker and writer who founded communism. He and his friend Friedrich Engels called on factory workers to seize factories and overthrow the rich.*

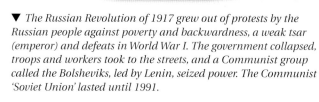

▲ *In 1949, led by Mao Zedong, Chinese Communists founded the People's Republic of China. Mao encouraged a violent 'Cultural Revolution' in the 1960s against all things traditional.*

▸▸	REMARKABLE REVOLUTIONS
1922	Sultan of Turkey overthrown; Turkey becomes a republic in 1923
1966	'Cultural Revolution' in China; Mao tries to destroy tradition and learning
1979	Islamic revolution in Iran; Ayatollah Khomeini overthrows the *shah* (emperor)
1989	Collapse of communism in Western Europe, with break-up of the USSR in 1991
1990	Nelson Mandela freed from prison; elected president of South Africa in 1994

POWERFUL WOMEN

Queen Hatshepsut of Egypt (about 1500 BC) was probably the earliest really powerful woman ruler. When she took over from her husband and son, she wore royal robes and a false beard, like a male pharaoh (king)! Later, Cleopatra ruled Egypt, but lost it to Rome. Another anti-Roman woman ruler was Boudicca, who led a British revolt against the Romans in AD 60. Some women rulers gained power through marriage, but England's formidable Queen Elizabeth I ruled alone. Catherine the Great, empress of Russia in the 1700s, ruled a huge empire, but Queen Victoria's was bigger, though she had less power.

◄ *Almost all of Egypt's rulers were men. The exception was Queen Hatshepsut. First she ruled with her husband, but after he died she had herself crowned as pharaoh and ruled alone from 1503 to 1482 BC. Hatshepsut famously sent a fleet of ships on an expedition to the Red Sea. The fleet returned with many wonderful gifts and wild animals.*

▼ *Queen Cleopatra of Egypt (69–30 BC) was the lover of Julius Caesar and then Mark Antony. Antony turned his back on Rome to be with her, but was defeated in battle by Augustus. After he killed himself, Cleopatra took poison.*

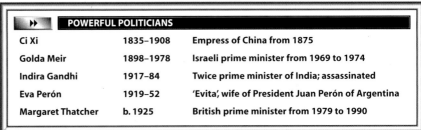

▶▶ POWERFUL POLITICIANS		
Ci Xi	1835–1908	Empress of China from 1875
Golda Meir	1898–1978	Israeli prime minister from 1969 to 1974
Indira Gandhi	1917–84	Twice prime minister of India; assassinated
Eva Perón	1919–52	'Evita', wife of President Juan Perón of Argentina
Margaret Thatcher	b. 1925	British prime minister from 1979 to 1990

▼ *Elizabeth I of England gave her name to the Elizabethan age – the age of playwright William Shakespeare and explorer Sir Francis Drake. During her reign (1558–1603) England became strong and prosperous. Elizabeth never married, for fear of handing control of her country to a man.*

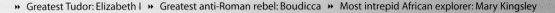
» Greatest Tudor: Elizabeth I » Greatest anti-Roman rebel: Boudicca » Most intrepid African explorer: Mary Kingsley

◀ *During the 1900s, Queen Victoria was head of the British Empire, the largest empire in the world at the time. She reigned for over 60 years, and her name was known in almost every country on Earth. She worked closely with her husband, Albert, who died in 1861.*

▶ *Roman Catholic nun Mother Teresa (born Agnes Gonxha Bojaxhiu in Macedonia in 1910) was admired for her tireless medical and missionary work among the poor of Calcutta in India. She died in 1997.*

▶ *Boudicca was queen of the Iceni, a British tribe who rose in revolt against the Roman invaders. In AD 60 the Romans moved into Iceni territory and Boudicca led an army, which burned London. A Roman counter-attack defeated her and she took poison to evade capture.*

▶▶ REMARKABLE QUEENS

Cleopatra of Egypt	69–30 BC	Lover of two famous Romans, Julius Caesar and Mark Antony
Eleanor of Aquitaine	1122–1204	Wife of Henry II of England, mother of kings Richard I and John
Elizabeth I of England	1533–1603	Ruled alone, refusing to marry, and defied the might of Spain
Marie Antoinette of France	1755–93	Wife of King Louis XVI, guillotined during the French Revolution
Victoria of Great Britain	1819–1901	Queen from age 18 until her death in 1901

◀ *Eva Perón (1919–52) was a powerful figure in Argentina, where she became known as 'Evita'. She was the politically active wife of President Juan Perón, elected in 1946, and worked alongside him until her death.*

▶ *Lady Diana Spencer's marriage (1981–96) to the Prince of Wales made her an international celebrity. As the self-styled 'People's Princess', she devoted herself to causes such as AIDS charities and banning landmines. Diana died in a car crash in 1997.*

MYSTERIES FROM HISTORY

Was England's King Richard III really a murderer? Did he order someone to kill his dead brother's two young sons in 1483, so he could take the throne himself? The fate of the 'Princes in the Tower' is just one of many tantalising mysteries from history. We may never know the answers to some of the riddles. But sometimes science solves a puzzle. Ever since the Russian Revolution of 1917, people have wondered whether all the daughters of the last tsar of Russia were murdered in July 1918, or whether one of the princesses escaped. In the 1990s, scientific tests on human remains proved that all were killed, solving just one of many mysteries.

▲ *The Russian royal family was murdered by Bolshevik communists in July 1918. The fate of Tsar Nicholas II, his wife Alexandra, and their children remained shrouded in mystery for years, until their remains were discovered and identified by DNA testing. They were given an official funeral in St Petersburg in 1998.*

AUSTRALIA

◀ *Who reached the North Pole first? Robert Peary claimed to have got there in 1909. His claim was challenged by another American, Frederick Cook, who said he got to the Pole a year earlier. Possibly neither did, because of navigation errors, but modern research suggests Peary got close to the Pole.*

▲ *Australia was unknown to Europeans before 1606, although the Aborigines had lived there for at least 50,000 years. However, sailors may have sighted 'Terra Australis Incognita' (Unknown Southland) 100 years earlier, because a mysterious landmass like it is shown on maps from the 1540s.*

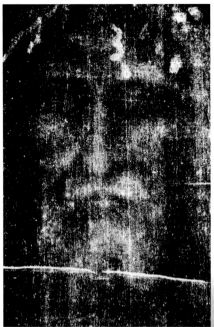

▶ *England's King Richard III (1483–85) is often blamed for the murder of his brother's two sons, but the case has never been proved. The elder boy was next in line to the throne after the death of his father, Edward IV. Richard kept the boys locked in the Tower of London for 'protection'. But neither boy was seen after 1483. Two skeletons were found in 1674.*

▼ *In 1872 the* Mary Celeste *left New York Harbor with ten people on board. A month later, a British ship crossing the Atlantic Ocean found the* Mary Celeste *drifting. When sailors went aboard, they discovered breakfast laid on the table and valuables still in the safe, but nobody there. No-one knows how or why all ten people disappeared.*

▲ *The Turin Shroud is a linen cloth, kept in Turin Cathedral in Italy. It appears to bear an image of a crucified man, seen most clearly in photographs. Some people believe it to be the burial cloth of Jesus. Others say it is a clever forgery. Scientific tests have cast doubt on the cloth's age, suggesting it dates from the 1300s, but the mystery remains unsolved.*

◀ *Atlantis was a legendary ancient island, said to have sunk beneath the ocean. The island of Thera, now called Santorini, in Greece, was destroyed about 3,500 years ago by a volcanic eruption and tidal wave. Maybe Thera, with its rich Minoan (Cretan) civilization, was Atlantis. The Greek philosopher Plato wrote that Atlantis was drowned because its people were wicked.*

» 7. Genghis Khan » 8. Spain » 9. Florence Nightingale » 10. Ferdinand Magellan » 11. The Hundred Years' War
» 18. Al Capone » 19. Adolf Hitler » 20. Boudicca

HISTORY *QUIZ*

Now that you have read all about the biggest and best in History, see if you can answer these 20 quiz questions! (Pictures give clues, answers at the top of the page.)

▲ *3. In which country was the ancient town of Çatal Hüyük discovered?*

▼ *4. A famous wooden horse was used by soldiers to enter which city?*

▼ *1. Which ship was found mysteriously sailing along with no people aboard?*

▶ *2. How many thousands of years ago did Homo sapiens first appear?*

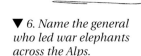

▼ *6. Name the general who led war elephants across the Alps.*

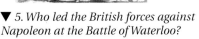

▲ *7. Who conquered the biggest-ever land empire?*

▼ *5. Who led the British forces against Napoleon at the Battle of Waterloo?*

◀ *9. What was the name of the 'lady with the lamp'?*

▼ *8. Which nation conquered the Aztec Empire in the 16th century?*

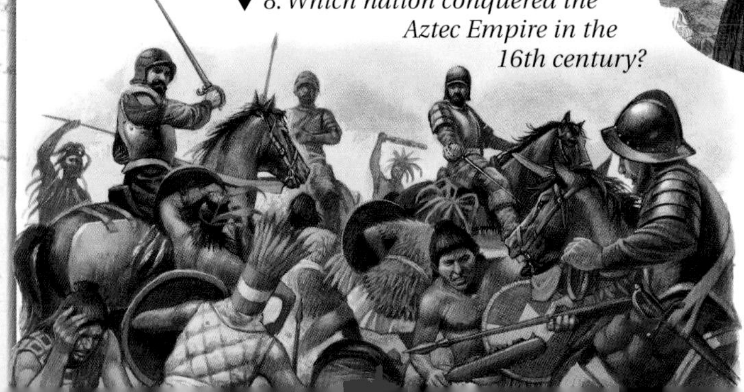

▶ *10. Who led the first sea voyage around the world?*

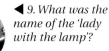

▲ 11. Which
was the longest war in history?

▼ 12. Che Guevara
was a communist
revolutionary in
which country?

▲ 13. In which World War I
battle did most
soldiers die?

◄ 14. In which
country was there a
revolution in 1917?

▼ 15. Who was the
first president of the
United States?

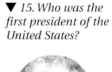

▲ 16. Name the first
explorer to reach the
South Pole.

▼ 18. Which
American gang-boss
was eventually jailed
for tax evasion?

▼ 20. Which queen revolted
against the Romans
in AD 60?

▲ 17. Which
leader was
known as the
'Great Soul'?

▲ 19. Who was
the leader of
Germany in
World War II?

INDEX

The publishers wish to thank the following artists
who have contributed to this book:
C.M. Buzer/Studio Gallante, Martin Camm, Jim Channell, Terry Gabbey,
Luigi Gallante/Studio Gallante, Alan Hancocks, Richard Hook, Terry Riley,
Martin Sanders, Rob Sheffield, Rudi Vizi, Mike White

The publishers wish to thank the following sources
for the photographs used in this book:
CORBIS: Page 24 (B/R) Bettmann; Page 26 (T/R) Bettmann;
Page 27 (B/L) Bettmann; Page 33 (B/R) Photo B.D.V; Page 35 (T/L) David Lees
All other photographs from Miles Kelly Archives